MILTON

Hi there!

My name is Milton. After being home for over a year and a half

(The VIRUS)

I said to myself "Milton, you need to get out and make some new friends and have some new adventures."

So, here I am reaching out to you.

I am 16 years old, in man years that is 112 years old!

So, you see, I am pretty darn old.

But, except for stiff legs, I am in good shape.

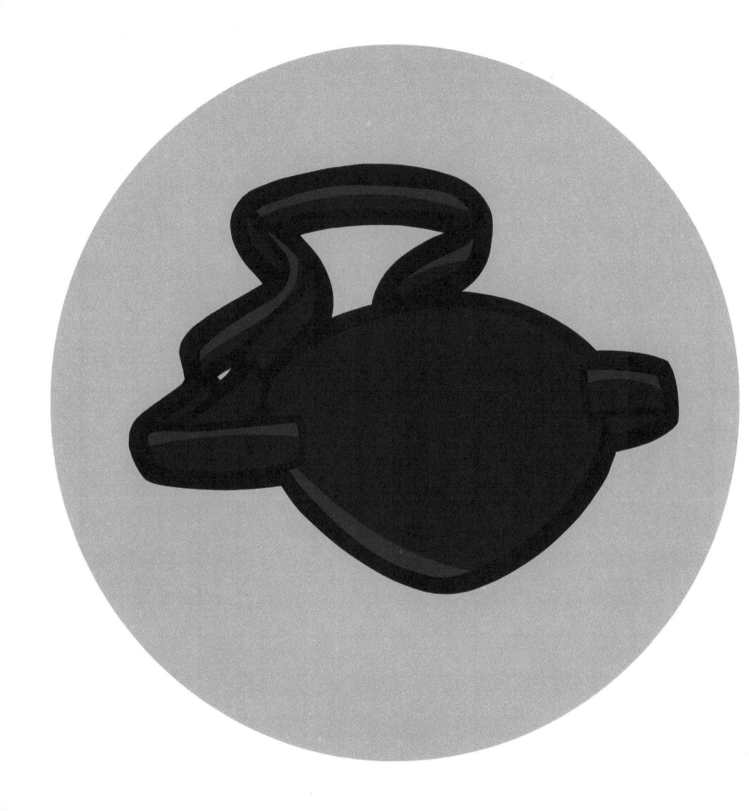

You may notice from my picture that I have only one eye.

Now, that is a story for another day!

It's NO BIG Deal for me. I lost it years ago.

I live in Washington D.C. on Capitol Hill, right near the United States Capitol.

Now the Capitol is a Big Deal! People come from all over the world to see it.

It is a very important place! For me though, it is just an everyday sight. I just walk through the neighborhood and mind my own business.

This summer my family said "We can travel again! Let's go on a vacation!"

   WHOOPEE!!!

They went to Florida. I went across the river to Virginia.

   WHAT???

I ended up a houseguest with a lady in Virginia.

I was not happy when my family left me.

The lady with gentle hands and a soft voice made me feel welcome.

We sat on her sofa and snuggled. I began to feel better.

I had to let her know who was the BOSS though.

I needed to stretch out my legs. She needed to curl up and give me more space.

Well, I guess to be honest. I do have a couple of issues. My family says I have separation anxiety. Well, I am not sure what that means but all I know is

"DON'T LEAVE ME ALONE!"

The very first night the Lady said "Bedtime Milton". She walked upstairs. I went to the stairs and looked up.

I don't do stairs.

Remember, Stiff Legs.

So, I began to whine until she came down and picked me up.

She had my bed on the floor, then she got in her bed. I sniffed the bed and walked away.

"Go to sleep, Milton," said the Lady.

"No Way" barked me.

She got it. Quick Learner!

She picked me up and, in the bed, I settled, legs out straight. She slept on the edge.

HONK

HONK

HONK

HONK

HONK

HONK

One night we had a real adventure. At 3:00 AM in the very middle of the night her car alarm went off. She grabbed me and then we flew down the stairs. Outside we went. The car was honking! The lights were flashing! It was crazy. I had been dreaming about chewing on a Big Dog Bone and grinding my teeth when this happened. My sleep is important. Remember I am 112 years old.

We went for lots of walks. Again, I had to take charge.

I would stiffen my legs and refuse to move when she went too far.

If, it was too hot I would just lie down and glare at her.

I like to be comfortable.

After all, Lady, I am 112 years old.

We met other dogs in her neighborhood.

They were fine,

I am used to being the Top Dog on Capitol Hill. With my age, 112 and experience I deserve respect.

I try to be dignified but then I met Jasper. He is the puppy, who lives next door.

He was squirming and wiggling and kissing me!

I was like Settle Down Kid! Learn Some Self Control!

A couple of times I forgot where she lived. The Lady lives in a townhouse. The houses all look the same. Remember, I only have one eye.

I would lie down outside the house next door and not move. The Lady said "wrong house Milton."

She just picked me up and home she went.

One day, I had a rather embarrassing moment. It was really the Lady's fault. I barked and pranced around to go outside.

She went upstairs to dress.

What was she thinking?

When you gotta go,

well, you gotta go!

You know how your Mom and Dad have alarm clocks. Maybe, you have one too! Well, I have a clock in my stomach. It doesn't ring but it starts to rumble every single day at exactly 3:30 PM. So, I need a snack. And, I do NOT MEAN 3:35pm. I MEAN 3:30 PM.

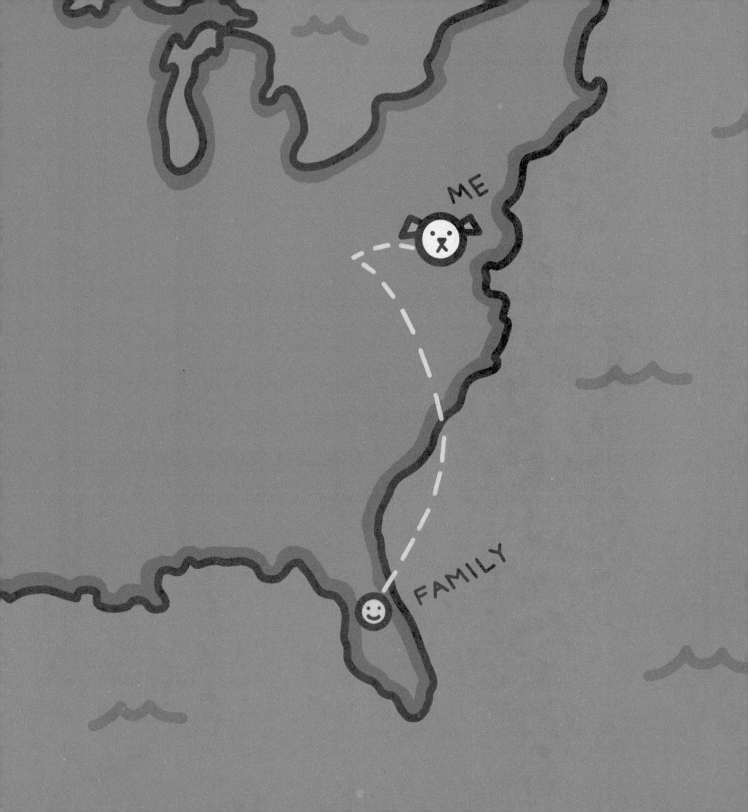

After ten days it was time for me to go. The Lady was packing my suitcase and said Milton, today you are leaving for home. I heard a little quaver in her voice. I looked at her and saw a little tear in her eye. Hmm this is interesting I thought.

When my family arrived it was

MILTON, MILTON, MILTON.

I think they thought I would run up all excited and wag my tail. Well, I turned my back to them, put my nose in the air and thought

LET THEM BEG!

Of course, I gave in, after all we are FAMILY. You just cannot stay mad at FAMILY. Off we went in the car and I thought about my time in Virginia with the Lady with the gentle hands and soft voice. It really had been an adventure and I really had made a very special friend.

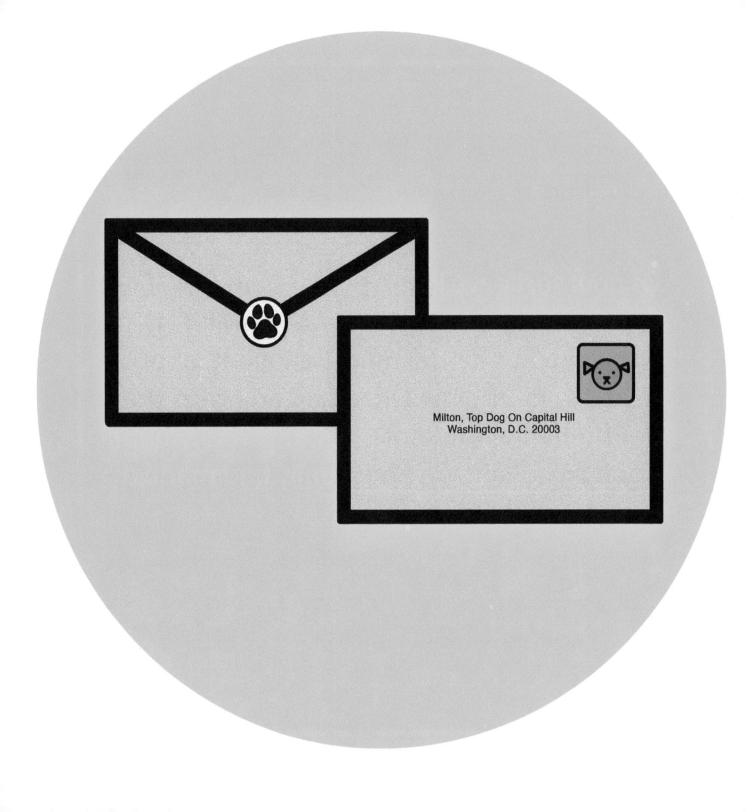

If you want to be my friend, jot me a note.

Milton, Top Dog On Capitol Hill

Washington, D.C.

20003

About the Author

Linda Bowles is a retired R.N., who graduated from The Ohio Valley General Hospital School of Nursing. She was born and raised in Steubenville, Ohio. Linda is the mother of two daughters and the grandmother of four. She now lives in Herndon, Virginia. Her love of children's books is well known to family and friends as she purchases one on every trip she takes. A photo of her and fellow travelers is placed in the book and saved for her grandchildren.

About the Illustrator

Julia Gonzales' love for art and illustration began in preschool when she and her mother would make crafts, paint and draw every day. That passion has grown into a successful freelance business that she works from her studio in sunny Orlando, Florida.

Her illustrations range from cartoons, book illustrations, logos, animations, website design, magazine editing, graphic design and of course this children's book.

CPSIA information can be obtained
at www.ICGtesting.com
Printed in the USA
BVHW021407231121
622345BV00011B/504

9 781665 541114